A Shared Understanding
of Ministerial Leadership

A Shared Understanding of Ministerial Leadership

Polity Manual for Mennonite Church Canada
and Mennonite Church USA

MennoMedia

Harrisonburg, VA

Library of Congress Cataloging-in-Publication Data

A shared understanding of church leadership: polity manual for Mennonite
Church Canada and Mennonite Church USA.
    pages cm
  Includes index.
  ISBN 978-0-8361-9900-0 (pbk. : alk. paper) 1. Mennonite Church Canada
—Government. 2. Mennonite Church USA—Government. 3. Christian
leadership—Mennonite Church Canada. 4. Christian leadership—Mennonite
Church USA. I. MennoMedia.
  BX8126.S53 2014
  262'.097--dc23
                        2014016272

A Shared Understanding of Ministerial Leadership:
Polity Manual for Mennonite Church Canada and Mennonite Church USA

© 2017 by MennoMedia, Harrisonburg, Virginia 22802. 800-245-7894.
    All rights reserved.
International Standard Book Number: 978-1-5138-0162-9
Printed in the United States of America
Cover design by Merrill Miller
Layout by Reuben Graham

Unless otherwise noted, Scripture text is quoted, with permission, from the
New Revised Standard Version, © 1989, Division of Christian Education of the
National Council of Churches of Christ in the United States of America.

The content for this book was sponsored jointly by Mennonite Church Canada
and Mennonite Church USA.

19 18 17 16 15   10 9 8 7 6 5 4 3 2

 MennoMedia

Table of Contents

Introduction

A common understanding of how we do things in the church—specifically in the area of leadership—is a service to local congregations, area conferences, and the denomination. Based on many ministry experiences, this book identifies and names the best path for the health of all involved. The intent of the content is not to be a rule book, nor is there any assumption that every possible ministry question is addressed in these pages. It is, however, our effort to build lasting relationships of respect and integrity between congregations, area conferences, and their credentialed leaders.

Healthy relationships know the value of talking about expectations and being intentional about identifying them early in the relationship. Regular review of these understandings—to see what might need to be renegotiated and adjusted to meet new realities—is a proactive way to retain a healthy relationship. Unknown and unspoken expectations lead to unnecessary frustrations and relational stress.

The content that follows is a revision of an earlier book, *A Mennonite Polity for Ministerial Leadership*. This significant work was done before the 2001 transformation process that birthed both Mennonite Church Canada and Mennonite Church USA. It has served our national churches well in creating shared understandings of how we do things in the church in the area of ministerial leadership. The former booklet offered a framework for understanding ministerial leadership beginning with the New Testament, the history of our different polities, and the process of coming together. It may be consulted for those who desire such a historical perspective.

Much in our world and the church has changed. Our agreed-upon understandings do well to reflect this. The revisions in this book are a way of naming the missional church we understand God is calling us to become.

Our prayer is that these efforts will help congregations and ministerial leaders to more fully live out our vocational calling, together. We are grateful to all the Mennonite Church Canada and Mennonite Church USA area-church/conference ministers, pastors, scholars, and other church leaders who gave of their insight and wisdom in the development of this document.

—Karen Martens Zimmerly, Nancy Kauffmann and Terry Shue,
   Denominational Ministers for Mennonite Church Canada and
   Mennonite Church USA

Note: In this binational document serving both Mennonite Church Canada and Mennonite Church USA, we have introduced the term *area conference* to speak of the regional part of the church, between the local congregation and the national church. This term is used for the *area church* and the *conference* in this document.

Section I: Theological Background for Ministry

Throughout the biblical narrative we see God moving in and through history, cultures, and peoples. At the coming of Jesus, the incarnation and full revelation of God, we see and understand anew God's passion for reconciliation with all of humanity and the world. Through the Holy Spirit's power we are loved, redeemed, called, and sent into this world to participate in God's mission of reconciling all people to God, humanity, and creation (Romans 8). This same Spirit transforms us and places us in communities where we discover the purpose of our lives and our place in God's mission. Personal transformation is the vital beginning point that leads ultimately to a life of engagement in the world that God desires to transform as well. Our response to all of God's initiative—past, present, and future—is the foundation for all Christian ministries.

Though there remain places and reminders of an earlier dominant Christian culture, post-Christendom experiences of reality are becoming more prominent in North American society. This growing reality challenges us to clarify our understanding of what it means to be the church in the world. This needed clarity reaches to very basic matters of the identity, ministry, and mission of the church. The church finds itself on the margins of society, with a drastically diminished scope of influence in the political and social powers that gave the church institutional strength for centuries. Ironically, just as the Christian church's institutional strength is eroding in the West, Mennonites have begun to reflect society's mainstream rather than the separatist tendencies of previous generations. These shifts are posing challenging questions for the church as God's primary agent of mission in the world.

In this new experience of reality, we believe God has called us to be a church whose identity, ministry, and mission is continually being formed at the intersection of Word (John 1:1) and world (John 1:10). This is a dynamic process which, when Spirit led, has profound implications for the calling, formation, identity, and function of leaders in the church.

In the post-Christendom context biblical models of leadership ministry reemerge as relevant and important. The five-fold ministry of Ephesians 4 (see section IV) will help congregations to identify and call out the gifts needed for church leadership in the emerging cultural shifts around us. Likewise, the missional model in Luke 10 portrays the *sent ones* as leaders going beyond their own contexts with experimental and imaginative ministries.

All followers of Jesus are called to ministry: as individuals, as part of a local community of believers, and as part of the wider church. Within this broad understanding of ministry, the Mennonite church recognizes leadership roles that may or may not be credentialed. These leadership roles are a means to something else, rather than ends in themselves. Christian ministry points beyond the church to the world as the focus of God's mission. Therefore, the goal of Christian leadership is to equip the church to participate in God's redemptive activity in the world.

This document describes the reasons why the church credentials persons who serve in pastoral ministry, congregational leadership, and other specialized leadership ministries. A credential is an approval for ministry granted to a person for a period of time. Credentialing is an action of the church, in response to the call of God and the leading of the Spirit in the congregation and the candidate's life. It is requested by the congregation, administered and held by the area conference, and granted to the ministering person in order to provide accountability and greater credibility to the recipient's ministry.

Ministry finds its basis in the New Testament

While the Old Testament offers numerous examples of God's calling forth and using of leaders, the models most applicable to the church today are found in the New Testament. The New Testament's language and images regarding ministry are both varied and complex. Literally dozens of words and images are used to describe the multifaceted dimensions of ministry: such as *servant, deacon, apostle, elder, presbyter, overseer, bishop, evangelist, shepherd*, and *pastor*.

In addition to special terms and images, several New Testament passages speak directly about leadership ministry. Ephesians 4, 1 Corinthians 12–14, and Romans 12 give special emphasis to the nature and place of spiritual and leadership gifts for the church. Each of these gifts given to the church is part of a larger whole. Each is incomplete in itself, but together they build up the body of Christ.

First Peter 4:10-11 stresses serving others as stewards of God's grace. Chapter 5:1-4 views Jesus Christ as the chief Shepherd and calls the elders to be shepherds of God's flock. Second Corinthians is devoted almost entirely to leadership ministry themes. Paul defends and discusses his calling as an apostle and his response to opposition. He puts forth such metaphors for ministry as "the aroma of Christ," "ambassador," and "agents of reconciliation." In addition to these passages, we also look to the actual ministry of the early church as in Acts and the Epistles.

It is in the ministry of Jesus that we find both meaning and a model for our ministry. Jesus' ministry derived from his relationship with God. This resulted in the conviction of his being both called and sent. In Jesus we see one who "made himself nothing, taking the very nature of a servant" (Philippians 2:7 NIV), obedient to God even unto death, yet ministering with authority, confidence, compassion, and competence. We see Jesus' ministry

- finding its center and authority in God (John 17:1-5);
- being responsible to God (John 17:6-12);
- proclaiming the kingdom of God (Luke 4:18-19);
- instructing in the way of God (Matthew 5–7); and
- bridging economic, cultural, and racial divides (Ephesians 2:14-22)

- confronting evil powers (Luke 11:14-20)
- calling persons to love (Matthew 5:43-48)
- demonstrating compassion (Mark 1:29-34)
- celebrating life (John 2:1-11)
- walking in prayerful relationship with God (John 5:16-27)
- calling persons to repentance and forgiveness of sins (Matthew 4:17; 9:2)
- respecting the freedom of others (Luke 18:18-25)
- empowering others for ministry (Matthew 16:17-19)
- calling persons to a response of commitment and discipleship (John 3:1-21).

Jesus' ministry and leadership was powerful yet not domineering, authoritative but not authoritarian. It was life giving, liberating, and loving even unto death. In John 20:21 Jesus declares to his disciples, "As the Father has sent me, so I send you." At the heart of this sending is the challenging, countercultural content of ministry, which is moral discernment; "If you forgive the sins of any, they are forgiven them; if you retain the sins of any, they are retained" (John 20: 23).

Called by God and informed by Jesus' ministry, all Christian ministry is incarnational, purposeful, and willing to risk. As a servant leader (Luke 22:26), Jesus taught his followers to minister in the name of Christ (Matthew 28:19-20), empowered by the Spirit of Christ (Acts 1:8), emboldened by the authority of Christ (Matthew 18:15-20). From such studies come the convictions that Christian ministry

- continues God's work of reconciliation through Jesus and is entrusted to the church;
- is a calling characterized by a life of compassion, holiness, and humility of spirit;
- is rooted in God's love and depends on the Holy Spirit's power to faithfully follow Jesus;

- recognizes that God's Spirit is already at work in every ministry context; and
- is dependent on others' gifts of the Spirit in order to represent and become the earthly body of Christ.

Ministry embodies the way of Jesus

The foundation of all ministry is the person of Jesus. His life, teaching, death, and resurrection form the gospel message. All followers of Jesus embody the way of Jesus in their local contexts. The person of Jesus and his good news shape the congregation's identity and witness.

In similar fashion, a leader's life is a personal journey of growth through spiritual disciplines and the practice of leadership. The leadership model of Jesus is to embody care for those in the community of faith, as well as care and concern for those outside the faith community. Such leadership influences the congregation, the surrounding community, and the world. Such leadership ministry produces communities that proclaim the life, death, and resurrection of Jesus and represent the kingdom of God.

Ministry is for all baptized believers

Jesus called his followers to active discipleship (Matthew 16:24) and sent them out into the world (John 20:21). The early church recognized that the call to conversion and discipleship was a lifelong journey with Jesus that would involve transformation through the faith community's communal practices of worship, ministry, and mission (Acts 2:42-47). Jesus sent 72 representatives out in pairs to the surrounding villages and towns with the message that characterizes God's reign; "Peace to this house!" (Luke 10:1-5). According to Ephesians 4:1-16, Christ gives different gifts to individuals for the building up of Christ's body so that God's people are prepared for service. This same pattern is described as the work of the Holy Spirit in 1 Corinthians 12 and as participating in the body of Christ in Romans 12. For the good news to spread, all baptized believers are ministers of the gospel in their daily lives.

Ministry takes on richly varied and diverse forms

In recent history Mennonite congregational leadership has mainly reflected New Testament functions in roles such as that of elder, deacon, bishop, and pastor. Each of these functions may be filled by individual persons or a team of people working together. These leadership functions help the congregation find overall direction, and they enable its many gifts and ministries to work together and participate fully in God's mission in the world. In hospitals, mental-health centers, educational institutions, businesses, and prisons, people also express the need and desire for the gospel of Christ, spiritual care, and loving community.

The Mennonite church in North America continues to grow in diversity of size, location, worship style, socioeconomic makeup, and culture. Congregations are on a continuum from traditional to experimental. New expressions of faith communities are developing unique leadership-ministry roles for their local contexts.

Growing diversity is helping the church once again recognize that additional New Testament leadership gifts need to be identified, valued, and adapted in order to live out its call of being God's sent ones in the world. Besides pastors or shepherds, we need apostles, prophets, evangelists, and teachers (Ephesians 4:11). Those with these gifts need to be called out, nurtured, and trained in Anabaptist theology and practice.

This document provides a Mennonite polity of leadership ministry that embraces a diversity of ministering roles and provides structure and guidance for three broad categories of leaders:

1. Congregational leaders such as elders, deacons, lay ministers, and congregational chairpersons who represent the members of the congregation and share responsibilities to lead the congregation with credentialed leaders

2. Credentialed ministers who provide leadership in a local and/or specific setting (pastors, chaplains, and others included in the five-fold ministries of Ephesians 4)
3. Leaders who provide oversight to area conferences, congregations, and pastors (e.g., national church leaders, area conference leaders, regional ministers)

Such a model allows for order, diversity, and creative movement of the Spirit. It understands authority to be both communal and individual. It expresses services to one another rather than lording it over others. It is marked by mutual accountability and personal responsibility for all persons in leadership, with each other and before the church's Lord.

The church calls out persons to offices of ministry

All believers are given gifts for ministry, and the Mennonite church values the *priesthood of all believers*. Each believer has direct access to God. All are called to share in the priestly role of interpreting Scripture, participating in mutual discipline and forgiveness, and being Christ's witness. The Mennonite church also recognizes that some members are called to specific offices of ministry. *Office of ministry* refers to those roles and functions

- where being continually open to transformation by the Spirit is embraced as the foundational and essential virtue that enables one to lead and teach others about God's desire for their lives;
- through which other members' gifts are discerned, called out, and developed to build up the church's capacity to join God's mission;
- to which persons are most often called and appointed on a continuing and long term basis;
- which are representative of a local congregation or the church body as a whole; and
- which carry a particular responsibility for leadership and oversight.

The offices of ministerial leadership belong to the church, not the individual. The congregation and the pastor together discern the gifts and character that will help the congregation join God's mission. By seeking wise counsel the individual can make a more reliable decision about whether to enter or to continue in the ministerial office. Such decisions should be made in prayer and in conversation with others in the Christian community.

As a church committed to God's vision of reconciling all persons to God in Christ and breaking down all dividing walls of hostility (Ephesians 2), Mennonite Church Canada and Mennonite Church USA affirm that God gives ministry gifts and calls persons to leadership ministries without regard to gender, race, ethnic/cultural origin, or social standing. The Mennonite church, as one community of God's people, calls out persons from this diversity as a sign of God's unity and love for the world (John 17:23). There is, therefore, no place in Mennonite ministry for discrimination on the basis of gender, race, social standing, or ethnic/cultural/national identity (Galatians 3:27-28; 1 Corinthians 12:4-6).

Ministry receives its authority from both God and the church

The authority for ministry in the New Testament is rooted in Jesus Christ, who received it from God (Matthew 28:18), and through the Holy Spirit empowers people to be ministers of good news. The church affirms the empowering call from God through Christ as essential for ministry. The church has a shared role in discerning the pastor's call, blessing it, and granting authority to the ministering leader. The church and its leaders are accountable both to God and to each other as they respond to the call of ministry and lead with authority.

So what is meant by authority? Jesus redefines authority (Mark 10:43-45) and therefore redefines how the church and its leaders are to lead. This authority for ministry consists of at least three interrelated realities: being, office, and task.

All followers of Jesus Christ are called to a life of obedience where God's will is done on earth as it is in heaven (Matthew 6:10). When our lives as individuals and a faith community give evidence to the grace, joy, and peace of God's healing and hope, this empowering witness gives authority to our *being.* This being dimension is both dynamic and foundational for pastoral ministry. A leader's being is expressed in character that develops through spiritual, emotional, and relational well-being. When a leader's ministry has growing spiritual depth, competency in ministry, and relational trust, the pastor's maturing character strengthens the authority that the church confers.

Office is a symbolic way of speaking about the representational role that a ministerial leader fulfills on behalf of the church. Authority for fulfilling the role is given to the position, not the person. When the church ordains or licenses a pastor, it places a person into a position that is already given authority. This office may be vacant or filled, but the authority remains with the office, not the individual.

Task refers to specific roles such as preaching, teaching, community engagement, administration, and pastoral care. There is a certain degree of authority that comes from both the person and the congregation associated with carrying out these tasks.

Leading with authority is to be in the name and spirit of Jesus and the New Testament Scriptures: "speaking the truth in love" (Ephesians 4:13) and "not lording it over" others (1 Peter 5:3 NIV). Pastors live into the authority that God and the church have given through serving, through maturing relationships, and through leadership that builds up the body of Christ. The result is a church which seeks the will of God together and grows in joining God's presence and mission in the world.

Understanding Ordination

The offices of ministry are a great treasure of the church. Through careful and prayerful discernment, the church joins God in calling people to leadership ministry. Ordination, then, is an act of the church that confirms those whom God and the church have called to particular roles of leadership ministry—both to build up the local body and to further engage the congregation in the mission of God. By ordaining these persons to leadership ministry, the church declares them caretakers of the gospel, shepherds of God's people, and agents of healing and hope for the world. Such leadership seeks to "equip the saints" so that they may "grow up . . . into Christ" and "be worthy of [their] calling" to be partners in God's mission (Ephesians 4:1-16).

The roots of ordination go back to the Old Testament. God instructed Moses to consecrate Aaron and his sons as priests for the congregation of God's people (Exodus 29; Leviticus 8–10). Over a period of seven days, Israelites observed a prescribed series of washings, clothings, anointings, sacrifices, meals, and offerings until in the end "Aaron lifted his hands toward the people and blessed them . . . and the glory of the Lord appeared to all the people" (Leviticus 9:22-23).

Although the New Testament gives no clear mandate for such a ceremony, it tells of numerous times when Jesus and the church gave their blessing and confirmation to persons called and sent to represent God and the church in service and witness. Examples include Luke 9:1-6 (mission of the twelve); Matthew 28:16-20 (commissioning the disciples); John 21:15-19 (Jesus' words to Peter); Acts 6:1-7 (seven chosen to serve); Acts 13:1-3 (Barnabas and Saul commissioned); Acts 1:12-26 (Matthias chosen to replace Judas); and 2 Timothy 1:6 (laying hands on Timothy).

Not until the third century AD was ordination to ministerial leadership described and defined as a specific act of the church in response to the biblical mandate that "all things should be done decently and in order" (1 Corinthians 14:40).

Schisms and heresies in the early Christian church revealed the need to order leadership so as to protect, maintain, and defend the apostolic faith. Following the advice in 1 Timothy 5:22, "Do not ordain anyone hastily," the church found it necessary to lend clarity to leadership roles and relationships within the community of faith.

The Anabaptist confessions of the 16th and 17th centuries (Schleitheim 1527, Dordrecht 1632, Cornelis Ris 1766) give little specific guidance as to either the meaning or the practice of ordination, yet there is evidence that the service of ordination was practiced.

Ordination in the commentary section of article 15 of the 1995 *Confession of Faith in a Mennonite Perspective* is "a one-time event, kept active by continuing service in and for the church."

What is ordination?

Ordination is a joint act of the congregation, the area conference, and the denomination, which call and appoint a member to ongoing leadership ministry in the life and mission of the church. The ordination act includes the covenant between the church and the person being ordained, the laying on of hands, and the prayer of blessing for ordination. When the church ordains a man or woman to leadership ministry, it intends to say at least the following:

1. We confirm the call of God to the person being ordained for leadership ministry within or on behalf of the church, and we affirm the person's response to God's call. It is a time of blessing and celebration by the church for God's gracious gifts to all, and it is part of the church's ministry.

2. We affirm the person for unique leadership gifts brought to the Christian community. We recognize

the investment in spiritual, relational, and intellectual growth for this role within the church. We affirm clarity of identity as shepherds of the church and servants of Jesus Christ (Acts 20:28, 1 Peter 5:2-4).

3. We identify the person being ordained as one who in some way represents God in a priestly role within the faith community where all are priests serving God (Revelation 1:6; 5:10). We recognize the role of spiritual leadership within the church as rooted in Christ, guided by the Holy Spirit, and lived out in the practice of Christian spiritual disciplines, ethical living, and humility.

4. We entrust an office of ministry to the person being ordained, and we empower the person to act as a representative of the church, with both the privileges and the responsibilities of this office. We recognize in this ministerial office an authority granted for leadership within the church. This authority is constantly sustained by evidence of competence, wisdom, character, and humility.

5. The congregation and the person ordained enter a covenant of a mutual accountability, support, respect, and care. The person covenants to live a life that has moral integrity, to be a faithful steward of the gospel, to lead with humility, to respect others, and to grow in ministry. The congregation covenants to pray for the ordained person, to give and receive counsel, to support the person's leadership ministry, and to recognize the authority of the office into which the pastor has been ordained.

6. We declare our trust in the person being ordained by providing a credential for leadership ministry to build up the church for service to the world (Ephesians 4).

Who is to be ordained?

The call to leadership ministry is in the context of one's new birth into a living and abiding relationship with God through Christ. Leadership ministry is anchored in one's primary call to follow Christ. The person to be ordained will be a member of a Mennonite congregation and affirm the current Mennonite confession of faith as a guide for faith and practice within the Mennonite church. When the church ordains members for particular leadership roles, the church confirms:

- those who reflect the biblical standards of Christian living, such as the fruit of the Spirit: "love, joy, peace, patience, kindness, generosity, faithfulness, gentleness, and self-control" (Galatians 5:22-23);
- those who believe that servanthood is taught by Jesus as the central, defining characteristic of all true leaders, and who strive to live it in their lives (Mark 10:42-45);
- those whose lives model the biblical expectations of leadership for pastors, bishops, deacons, and elders (1 Corinthians 4:1-13; 12:1–14:40; 1 Timothy 3:1–6:19; and 2 Timothy 1:3–3:8; Titus 2:1–3:11; 1 Peter 5:1-11); and
- those called to special tasks and leadership ministries in and for the church (Romans 12:6-8; 1 Corinthians 12:1-31; Ephesians 4:11-13).

Ordination is designated for persons in pastoral ministries in the congregation, as well as other leadership ministries in specialized settings. Ordination is not necessarily appropriate, however, just because a person is employed by an institution owned by, or related to, the church.

Affirming that in Christ "there is no longer Jew or Greek, there is no longer slave or free, there is no longer male and female; for all of you are one in Christ Jesus" (Galatians 3:28), gender, race, social standing, or ethnic/cultural/national identity will not determine who is acceptable for ordination.

Implications of ordination

The Mennonite church has traditionally rejected the view that ordination is a sacrament that effects a change in the person being ordained. But insofar as persons are always affected and changed by covenant experiences, ordination may become a life-shaping and identity-giving moment. An ordained leader is empowered to act and speak on behalf of the church in many settings while in a leadership-ministry position. Although accountable to the church for the way in which he or she holds the privilege, an ordained pastor is granted authority to represent the church both within and beyond the community of faith.

Ordination offers a leadership-ministry assignment from which the person seeks to fulfill his or her calling. While ordination is a high calling for a few in the church, it is not a holier status but a place from which to live and work for the church.

Traditionally ordination has been understood as a lifetime commitment and therefore not a repeatable act. Ordained persons are to be guided by high ethical standards and accountable to the area conference holding their ordination credential, whether or not they are currently in a leadership-ministry assignment. Ordained persons who reach retirement age and discontinue active leadership ministry retain their ordination but no longer hold an office of ministry in the congregation. Retired pastors and other ordained persons will limit their leadership ministry within the congregation, unless invited by the current pastor. They continue to be accountable to the area conference that holds their credentials and to the congregations where they have membership. This standard also applies to area-conference ministers and national-church staff who are credentialed.

Section II: Qualifications for Ministry

Ministry is a calling to bear fruit in God's service. A life-giving and maturing ministry grows out of a personal, growing faith in Christ. Qualifications for ministry fall into four major categories: personal character, calling, function, and formation/training.

God calls and the church responds by establishing and nurturing settings for ministry. The church is, therefore, finally responsible for the settings in which pastors lead the church. It is expected that any person called to serve in such an office will hold membership for at least one year in a Mennonite congregation and give clear evidence of a deep commitment to that community of believers. Pastors from other Christian faith traditions will enter a discernment process with the congregation and area conference in which their membership is held, to determine their compatibility in leading a Mennonite congregation. The national-church offices, in collaboration with area-church leaders, share a protocol for bringing persons from other faith traditions into leadership in Mennonite congregations.

Ephesians 4 names leadership gifts of apostles, prophets, evangelists, pastors, and teachers in order for the church to be prepared for ministry and grow in maturity. No one person will have all of these leadership gifts and skills made available by Christ for ministry in the church. Thus, the qualifications for ministry recognize that specific skills and gifts will be identified in individuals and matched to ministries best suited to them.

Personal Character: Relationship to God, to Self, and to Others

Qualifications for ministry begin with one's new birth into a living and abiding relationship with God through Christ. Foundational to ministry is a commitment to the way of Christ and the church through believers baptism, membership covenant with a Mennonite congregation, and affirmation of the current Mennonite confession of faith. A genuine disciple of Christ is one who commits to walk with Christ. This commitment is expressed in a dynamic and growing faith through consistent and regular devotion to the Scriptures, prayer, fellowship with other believers, obedience to Christ's commands, and willingness to give and receive counsel in Christ's body.

The New Testament's pastoral epistles set a high standard of character qualifications for a variety of leadership positions within the church (1 Timothy 3; 1 Peter 5). Apostles like Peter and Paul provide a picture of leaders as passionate and committed disciples, yet leaders who are not perfect. These Scriptures call every leader to live a committed life of integrity, holiness, and willingness to confess one's sin and humanness, recognizing that both confession and humanness are dependent on God's grace.

Mennonite Church Canada and Mennonite Church USA celebrate the increasing ethnic diversity of the church and proclaim that in Jesus the dividing wall of hostility between races has been destroyed (Ephesians 2:14). Even while we see this diversity as a gift from God, we sadly acknowledge the sin of racism in the church. Racism thwarts relationships and diminishes the church. Leaders will strengthen their ministry and their congregations through intentional efforts to celebrate diversity, seek to undo racism, and develop intercultural competencies.

A ministering person with a healthy self-image demonstrates realistic self-appraisal together with emotional stability and a clear sense of self-worth. This self-worth finds its source in Christ.

A leader's life also provides evidence of personal character being transformed into Christlikeness. Evidences of such personal transformation include the fruit of the Spirit (Galatians 5:22-26) and the blessings of the Christian character described in the Beatitudes of Matthew 5. An attitude of joy, humility, openness, and integrity—founded on the transforming love of God, nurtured by following Christ, and empowered by the Holy Spirit—describes the person's developing character.

Ability to cope with stress and conflict is evident in a leader's personal life. Flexibility, adaptability, and maturity are reflected in the person's response to life's difficulties and trials. Growing understanding of self and ability to assess and manage one's emotions and functioning will equip the leader to live in times of stress in ministry.

A kind and friendly nature as well as the ability to speak the truth in love are expected of those called to the ministry. Matthew 18 provides guidance for caring and accountable relationships in the church community. It gives a model for addressing broken relationships with generous forgiveness and mercy, so that discipleship rather than conflict is the focus of community life.

God's Calling: Through the Person and by the Church

Ministry includes a personal, inner calling to ministry and an outer calling and affirmation by the church. The inner calling from God comes through a path of discernment, testing one's own heart and mind, and receiving a sense of personal confirmation. For some the journey is relatively short, and for others it is longer and may come through the testing of the early years of ministry. This process involves addressing questions such as:

- Do I find myself with a sense of deep love for the community of faith, despite the challenges and complexities?

- Is it common for me to be asked by others to be in positions of influence?
- When I am helping the church grow in mission, is it joyful for me and those with whom I am working?
- When I name the places where God's Spirit is at work, do others recognize them as well?

Other questions that must be resolved in discerning a call to ministry involve awareness of the shadow side of ministering personalities. For example:

- Do I have a spirit of servanthood, or am I subtly tempted by power?
- Do I have a proper sense of the nature of the work, or am I looking for prestige, recognition, and approval?

The candidate for ministry will begin to have a clearer sense of the responsibilities involved. These include the self-discipline and motivation required to remain faithful to the task of the call as well as to the call itself. With a growing sense of the inner call, there is alignment between one's personal gifts, attitudes, expectations, and personal desires; and the requirements, expectations, and demands of the call.

A person's call to ministry also occurs within the body life of the church. A person does not appoint him- or herself to the ministry—one is chosen by the church. By affirming a person's strengths and gifts, the congregation confirms the individual's inner call to ministry. The congregation affirms that the person is a member in good standing of the community of believers and has demonstrated leadership capabilities. There are times when the church will recognize that the gifts of the person are not those for pastoral ministry and therefore will not affirm the inner call.

Congregations are called to be open to the Spirit's movement within their life, and faithful in calling out God's gifts for building up the body. This will mean that at times the congregation will initiate an outer call with an individual before the person senses an inner call. In such cases the individual is invited to respond to the call of the congregation and test whether there is also an inner call from God.

The area conference and national church participate in discerning and validating a call through involvement in the ministry placement process, use of the Ministerial Leadership Information form, and guidance of the credentialing process.

Qualifications Related to Function

The New Testament names a diversity of gifts, including leadership gifts, which are given to the church in order to build up Christ's body in love and embody God's love in the world. The Mennonite church has adapted its leadership patterns from time to time. In recent generations the focus has been on three expressions of leadership: the (ordained) pastor and other congregational leaders at the congregational level, oversight leadership from the area conference and national church, and the teacher function in both the congregation and the wider church.

Identifying and developing new expressions of the gifts of apostles, prophets, and evangelists will strengthen and complement current leadership functions in guiding the church toward greater maturity. The following ministry expressions are found in Ephesians 4:11-13:

- **Apostle** (catalyst/visionary)—The focus of this gift is on the future: being sent to develop new possibilities for extending the gospel in new contexts, to form new leaders, and to network with others in new contexts.
- **Prophet** (challenger/truth teller)—The focus of this gift is transmitting both the hard messages and the encouraging messages of God, so that the church can discern its context and respond by obeying God's will, speaking the truth, and following God's way.

- **Evangelist** (communicator)—The focus of this gift is communicating clearly and sharing the good news of the gospel so that people respond and choose to follow Jesus Christ, as well inviting other believers to join in sharing the good news.
- **Pastor** (equipper)—The focus of this gift is fostering a healthy faith community that nurtures and equips growing disciples who join God's mission in the world.
- **Teacher** (reflective practitioner)—The focus of this gift is understanding and explaining with knowledge, wisdom, and insight so that the church remains biblically grounded in its Christian life and witness.

The ability to administrate and organize—including the ability to plan, solve problems, delegate authority, motivate people, and evaluate—are also important leadership skills. Administrative and organizational skills increase in importance as the size of the ministry setting grows. They are vital in carrying out leadership roles.

Together, the congregation and the person called to ministry will identify how the leader's gifts can be used to equip the congregation to fulfill its vision. A leader will have strengths in some of these functions and, together with the congregation, will call out others with complementary leadership gifts so that the congregation will grow in maturity and in every way into Christ. Some congregations may call several individuals with various gifts to form a leadership-ministry team.

Educational Qualifications

Since ministry involves both an inner and an outer call, some leaders will begin ministry with pastoral training while others may have little or no formal pastoral training as their call begins with the congregation's outer call. Although leaders come with diverse levels of educational preparation, specific training for pastoral ministry remains important.

The Ministerial Credentialing, Competencies, and Education document names six areas of leadership formation that all Mennonite pastors are to develop throughout their life of ministry. The six core competencies are biblical story, Anabaptist theology, Christian spirituality, self-awareness, missional engagement, and leadership. While the master of divinity degree is the recommended standard for pastoral ministry, it is equally important for a pastor to be willing to grow and learn. Continuing education is the expected standard of practice for all pastors. It is vitally important to sustain ministry.

During the credentialing process, the area conference will identify growth areas and will provide educational opportunities or point the candidate to specific courses offered by one of our schools. The schools of Mennonite Church Canada and Mennonite Church USA provide pastoral-ministry training programs and a variety of excellent continuing-education opportunities. Seeking out such opportunities is a practice of healthy, active, and growing pastors.

Section III: Calling, Covenants, and Credentials in Ministry

The purpose of polity is to create a common understanding of standards and practices for church leadership so that God is glorified through the church's ministry and witness. While all members are ministers, this polity describes leaders (most commonly pastors) who are given authority to lead a congregation or give oversight to ministry by the area conference and the national church.

Covenants, which are made voluntarily, lie at the heart of Anabaptist understandings of the church. As Mennonites we desire to live with each other in relationships of mutual accountability, respect, and care. Such connections help us be accountable to each other for our life and mission. "You are the body of Christ and individually members of it" (1 Corinthians 12:27). All members make a covenant at the time of baptism. Both the installation and the credentialing of a pastor are covenanting services between the pastor, the congregation, the wider church, and God.

This leadership polity understands the relationship between a congregation and its leaders—and also the relationships between congregations within the area conference and the national church—to be a covenant before God. The relationship, built on promises made, is one of interdependence and mutuality. This covenant is affirmed each time a congregation joins the area conference and national church. It is made real in the ongoing life of the church as it lives out its common confession of faith and as it carries out ministries that were decided upon jointly. The governance aspect of polity flows out of this understanding and respect for covenant.

Governance authority granted to leaders, then, is in the context of this larger covenant between the congregation, area conference, and national church. Authority is built on a strong sense of mutual accountability (Hebrews 13:17). Those chosen to lead are given support and are accountable to others in the church.

The ministerial-leadership polity that grows out of this covenant relationship recognizes three offices of ministry:

1. congregational leadership
2. pastoral leadership
3. oversight ministries of the area conference and national church

Normally pastors and those called to positions of oversight are ordained, while those called to congregational roles such as deacon and elder are usually not ordained. Congregations may choose to recognize their congregational leaders by commissioning them for their task.

Mennonite polity is one of a number of church polities. Church polities are on a continuum from hierarchical (with authority centralized in a few people) to congregational (where the primary decision-making authority is within the local congregation). On this continuum are three classic approaches: episcopal, presbyteral, and congregational. These approaches are expressed below in generalities for contrast:

- **Episcopal** polity has a hierarchical structure in which decisions are made by one person or by a few people (bishops). These decisions are then passed on with little if any input from the local faith community.
- **Presbyteral** polity gives leadership authority to a presbytery, which is a group of ordained leaders and congregational members who consult broadly and represent a group of congregations. Decisions made at the local level are subject to revision by higher bodies, such as the synod (a broader regional group) and the general assembly.

- **Congregational** polity describes a local approach to authority, in which decisions are made by the whole local congregation meeting to discern together, or by as many of them as choose to be involved. Regional bodies generally have only advisory power in relationship to a local congregation.

Each of these organizational styles—and various styles in between—has both strengths and weaknesses. Even with different histories and traditions, Mennonite polities have usually been found on the congregational end of the spectrum.

Within this continuum a Mennonite polity respects and takes seriously the congregation, and at the same time understands church to include the larger church family of area conferences, national-church bodies, and the global Mennonite church. Authority is shared within the local faith community, as well as with area-conference and denominational leaders; it is found in no one person. In practice, this authority is exercised in various circles through the granting and holding of credentials, through membership covenants and guidelines, through confessions of faith, and through the discernment of God's people. Such a polity is intended to serve not only the ministerial leadership of the congregation but also the ministerial leadership of area conferences and of Mennonite Church USA and Mennonite Church Canada.

Leadership Ministries—To Strengthen the Local Congregation

Congregational leaders

Congregational leaders—such as elders, deacons, lay ministers, and church board members—are chosen from the congregation because they demonstrate gifts for ministry, collaborative leadership, and a growing Christian faith. Some of these leaders may become part of a leadership-ministry team to assist in setting a vision for the congregation, assessing the local context for ministry, providing pastoral care, and providing spiritual oversight of the congregation. In some settings these congregational leaders also serve a governance role by giving oversight and accountability to the pastor. It is extremely important that the pastor and congregational leaders respect each other and work together for the good of the congregation and its witness to the community.

Boundaries and connections: Congregational leaders complement the pastor's ministry and are accountable to the congregation through periodic reviews. The goal is that every congregation experience committed, caring, spiritual leadership.

Pastoral leadership

Pastors who are credentialed by the area conference serve in the congregation to which they are called. Their tasks may include preaching, teaching, outreach, pastoral care and counseling, worship and formation (including baptism, communion, weddings, funerals, and equipping all members for ministry), and other activities that encourage congregational health and growth.

Boundaries and connections: Pastors respect each member of the congregation in which they serve. They are accountable to the congregation through the appropriate leadership structure to help the congregation fulfill its mission. They are credentialed and supported by the area conference for pastoral leadership in that congregation, and they are willing to receive the counsel of the area-conference minister. Pastors are supportive of other pastors and, where possible, meet together on a regular basis for prayer, mutual care, and encouragement.

Oversight ministries (area conference and national church)

Each area conference appoints area-conference ministry staff to serve in oversight ministries to local congregations. The understanding of the oversight role is grounded in the New Testament's pastoral epistles. The area-conference ministry staff offers pastoral support to the pastors and congregations within the area conference. The area-conference ministry staff relates to the credentialing body of the area conference and carries out its policies. The area-conference ministry staff participates in the credentialing process and with pastoral transitions, establishing guidelines for leadership ministry, and continuing-education opportunities. The area-conference ministry staff is accountable to the area conference through the structure established by that particular area conference. The overall focus of the area-conference ministry staff is to assist and challenge the pastors and local congregations to be fully engaged in God's activity in the world by providing resources, counsel, networking, and encouragement.

At the national-church level, an office for ministerial leadership will provide overall direction, coordination, and support to the pastoral-leadership system and to ministerial persons serving the church. The national office is responsible for providing resources (guidelines for ministry, ministerial-transition materials, and information services) and assistance (consultation and in-service training) to those persons in area conferences who provide oversight and care for the pastor-congregation system.

The office of ministerial leadership will supply procedures for granting ministerial credentials. It plans settings for area-conference ministers to unify practice in granting and maintaining credentials and to receive professional training and development. The national-church leadership offices keep files or profiles of those who carry ministerial credentials, and list each person's status and current service location in MennoData, the binational database for credentialed persons. The office of ministerial leadership is accountable to the churchwide gathering of area conferences through whatever governance structure has been established by the national church.

Boundaries and connections: Credentialed personnel at the offices of the national church and area conference respect each other's roles. They work together for the well-being of these wider church bodies, congregations, and those in ministerial positions. They are also intentional about being rooted within a local Mennonite congregation for the purposes of Christian fellowship, spiritual nurture, relational support, and healthy accountability.

Types of Credentials and How They Are Received

Leadership-ministry credentials are granted to those persons who sense a call to leadership ministry; are affirmed by their congregation for their gifts, character, and commitment; and are approved by the area-conference leadership-credentialing body. A person who senses God's call to long-term ministry with youth follows the same licensing and ordination procedure as for other congregational pastors. A person who senses God's call to long-term ministry with seniors, Christian formation, or other areas designated by the calling congregation may follow the same credentialing procedure.

Women and men may be granted credentials for Christian ministry that includes pastoral ministry in the congregational setting (lead, associate, assistant, youth, and co pastor) and ministry connected to other organizations (chaplains, teachers, counselors, mission workers, and area-conference and national staff). These credentials are granted by the area conference only for those who have a place of service. The credentials are recognized by all Mennonite Church Canada and Mennonite Church USA congregations and by area-conference and churchwide organizations. The credentialed person is accountable to the area conference for their ministry credential.

Licensing toward ordination

This ministerial license grants the person all the privileges and responsibilities accorded to an ordained person, except to ordain someone else. The license is usually issued for a minimum of a two-year period for the purpose of testing the inner and outer call to ministry. Further discerning of ministerial gifts, abilities, and aptitude may or may not lead to ordination. The license may be extended for another period of time if more discernment time is needed. The license credential ends when the person is ordained or is no longer serving in the present ministry assignment. The pastoral status of an assignment that ends is listed on MennoData as *expired*. A license for ministry is not transferable to another area conference or denomination.

To request a license for ministry, the following items should be submitted to the area-conference leadership-credentialing body:

a. a letter of request from the candidate's congregation for the person to be licensed (for a specialized ministry, a letter from the congregation and from the organization served is required);

b. a copy of a new or updated Ministerial Leadership Information form; and

c. other documents as requested by the credentialing body.

These materials are reviewed by the leadership-credentialing body prior to a personal interview with the candidate. This body will respond by either approving or denying the request for licensing. Using the six core competencies (biblical story, Anabaptist theology, Christian spirituality, self-awareness, missional engagement, and leadership) to enhance the person's ministry, the committee may assign reading, academic courses, or other requirements to be completed during the licensing period, prior to consideration for ordination. In addition, the committee will assign an experienced pastor within the Mennonite church to serve as a pastoral mentor to the person for the length of the licensing period. Recognition of the person's licensing usually happens during the congregation's worship service. An area-conference representative will be present to install and license the pastor.

Ordination for ministry

Ordination is a long-term, leadership-ministry credential granted by the church. Ordination may follow a period of licensing. Ordination is the appropriate credential for all pastors, area-conference ministry staff, chaplains, missionaries, evangelists, those serving as the national-office ministers, and those determined by the church to have a continuing ministerial-leadership role in, and on behalf of, the church. Ordination to the church's office of ministry grants to the person the full range of ministerial privileges and responsibilities.

Ordination normally follows the period of licensing, with initiation of the process before the license expires. Preparation for ordination will include assessment of and reflection on the person's ministry: within the congregation, with the area-conference minister, and with the pastoral mentor.

The area conference assists the congregation in the discernment and ordination process. The appropriate leadership groups in the congregation and the area conference work together with the candidate to discern readiness for ordination. While the area conference is responsible for the ordination credential, the area conference needs counsel from the congregation and pastor in order to make a good decision. Information is gathered relative to the six core competencies through interviews, references, and written material.

To request ordination for ministry, the following items should be submitted to the area-conference leadership-credentialing body:

a. a letter of request from the candidate's congregation for the person to be ordained, including a brief report of their discernment process;

b. a statement by the candidate concerning the meaning of ordination, its privileges and responsibilities, and the mutually understood accountability relationships;

      c. a written report and statement of support from the pastoral mentor (for persons in specialized ministry, a written statement from the organization is required);

      d. a theological statement or response as requested by the area-conference committee,

      e. a new or updated Ministerial Leadership Information form; and

      f. other documents as requested by the credentialing body.

These materials are studied by the appropriate area-conference committee prior to a personal interview with the candidate. The congregational leadership appoints a representative to participate with the candidate in the interview with the area-conference committee. This committee will follow with its response, either affirming or denying the request for ordination.

Upon approval of the ordination, an ordination service is planned by the congregation in consultation with the area conference and the person to be ordained. The area-conference representative will lead the ordination service to symbolize the covenant relationship between pastor, congregation, and wider church. Usually a special worship service is planned, and the wider church is invited to participate in the celebration.

Licensing for specific ministry

This credential is time specific, location specific, or ministry-role specific. It is usually not intended to move toward ordination. This credential is for a person who does not sense a personal call to ordained ministry. The person is called from within the congregation to serve in a specific leadership assignment, and may receive this credential. The credential continues as long as the person is engaged in a leadership-ministry assignment within the congregation, or another specialized leadership ministry (church planters, chaplains, area-church and national-church staff). While this credential is given to a person who may be serving in an institution other than the congregation, the licensing request from the institution should be processed with the congregation and the area conference. This credential is not transferable to another area conference. An individual with a license for specific ministry and the congregation may come to a new understanding about the call to ministry on the individual's life. In this case the congregation may call for ordination.

This ministerial license grants the person all the privileges and responsibilities accorded to an ordained person, except to ordain someone else. This ministerial credential is issued for the duration of a particular term of service. It may be limited in time, position, role, or geographical location; and it is not transferable to another area conference or denomination. Once the assignment is completed, this license ends, and the pastoral status on MennoData will be listed as *expired*.

To request the license for specific ministry, the following items should be submitted to the area-conference leadership-credentialing body:

a. a letter of request from the candidate's congregation for the person to be licensed for specific ministry (for a specialized ministry, a letter from the congregation and from the organization served is required); and

b. a copy of the Ministerial Leadership Information form.

These materials are studied by the appropriate area-conference leadership-credentialing body prior to a personal interview with the candidate. This body will follow with a response, either approving or denying the request for licensing for specific ministry. Using the six core competencies (biblical story, Anabaptist theology, Christian spirituality, self-awareness, missional engagement, and leadership) to enhance the person's ministry, the committee may also suggest additional reading or academic courses. In addition, the committee will assign an experienced pastor within the Mennonite church to serve as a pastoral mentor to the person for the first two years of the licensing period.

A licensing service usually takes place during the congregation's worship service. An area-conference representative will be present to license the person.

Commissioning

Commissioning is a blessing given by a congregation for persons performing specialized tasks in the congregation, for missionaries, or for Christian service workers. It is congregation based and does not require area-conference action.

Maintaining ministerial credentials

The area conference holds the credentials of all persons who are licensed toward ordination, ordained, or licensed for specific ministry serving in that area conference. Each area conference is responsible to maintain up-to-date records of all credentials on MennoData. For the health of pastors and congregations, the area conference provides an accountability structure and resources for all credentialed persons in their area conference. Once a year the national offices ask the area conferences to update their records using the following categories on the MennoData system.

Credentials by ministerial role
I. Oversight of Pastoral Ministries

- A. Licensed toward Ordination—not normally used for Oversight Ministry IA
- B. Ordination
   1. Ordained and serving as a national office minister IB1
   2. Ordained and serving as an area-conference minister or youth minister IB2
   3. Ordained and serving in a regional-ministry position (regional area conference minister, overseer, bishop, or district elder) IB3
- C. Licensed for Specific Ministry IC

II. Pastoral Ministries and Wider Church Leadership

A. Licensed toward Ordination—initial ministry role within denomination IIA

B. Ordination
   1. Ordained and serving as a lead pastor or copastor in a congregation IIB1
   2. Ordained and serving as an associate, assistant, or youth pastor in a congregation IIB2
   3. Ordained and serving in a specialized setting
      a. Chaplain or pastoral counselor IIB3a
      b. Church planter, transitional pastor, mission or service assignment IIB3b
      c. Area-conference or national-church executive leadership IIB3c
      d. Teacher in a Mennonite Church Canada/USA educational institution IIB3d

C. Licensed for Specific Ministry IIC
   1. Licensed and serving as a lead pastor or copastor in a congregation IIC1
   2. Licensed and serving as an associate, assistant, or youth pastor in a congregation IIC2
   3. Licensed and serving in a specialized setting
      a. Chaplain or pastoral counselor (usually a chaplain will be licensed toward ordination or ordained) IIC3a
      b. Missions or service assignment IIC3b
      c. Area-conference or national executive leadership IIC3c
      d. Teacher in a Mennonite Church Canada/USA educational institution IIC3d

III. Congregational Leadership Ministries

Congregational leaders who are called to serve may be commissioned by the congregation. A commissioning is a special blessing by the congregation but is not considered a credential by an area conference or the wider church. It is not recorded in MennoData.

Categories of credentials

License toward Ordination (LTO)—A license granted for the purpose of discerning ministerial gifts, abilities, and aptitude—usually for a minimum of two years. It can be renewed for an additional term if more time for discernment is needed, unless the person moves to ordination or the assignment ends. During the licensing period, the pastoral status is *active*. The pastoral status for an assignment that ends is listed as *expired*.

Ordination for Ministry:

Active (OAC)—The credential held by those serving in a leadership-ministry assignment.

Active without Charge (OAW)—The credential held by those not presently holding a ministry assignment. This status is good for a period of up to three consecutive years, after which the credential status usually becomes *inactive*. Occasionally a conference may have a special reason to extend that status for a longer period of time.

Inactive (OIN)—The credential held by those who have been without a ministerial assignment for more than three consecutive years. This credential is not valid for performing ministerial functions. The area conference that holds this credential is not responsible for the actions of a person so recognized. If, subsequently, an invitation to a ministerial assignment is received, the area-conference leadership-credentialing body will be informed, and an interview will be conducted to decide whether to reactivate the ordination credential.

Retired (ORE)—The credential held by those who have retired from active ministry. This credential is valid for performing ministerial functions and is to be exercised in consultation with the area conference. A person who had retired at one time but then is invited to a ministry assignment will have the pastoral status changed to *active.*

Probation (OPR)—The credential held by those having a ministry assignment who are placed under close supervision for a specified period of time in order to determine whether the credential will be continued. At the conclusion of the probationary period, it is determined whether the credential becomes *active, suspended,* or *terminated.*

Suspended (OSU)—The ministry credential is laid aside for a specified period of time for disciplinary reasons. At the end of the suspension period, a determination is made as to whether the credential moves to *probation, active,* or *terminated.* Suspended credentials are not valid for performing ministerial functions.

Terminated (OTE) (previously Withdrawn)—The status given when the area conference has actively removed the credential because of a disciplinary action. The individual will no longer have an ordination credential.

Withdrawn (0W1) (previously Terminated)—The status given when a ministry credential is ended for nondisciplinary reasons. This status is also given to a pastor who no longer is affiliated with Mennonite Church Canada and Mennonite Church USA. The individual will no longer have an ordination credential.

Deceased (ODE)

Licensed for Specific Ministry (LSM)—The credential granted for the duration of a particular term of service, which is limited in time, position, role, or geographical location. When the assignment ends, the pastoral status in MennoData becomes *expired.*

The transfer of credentials

When an ordained person moves to another area conference, the receiving area conference requests the transfer of the credential. The area conference in which the pastor has served is responsible to review the pastor's experience and determine whether the pastor's credential is in good standing for transfer. Within MennoData the only credential that can be transferred is an ordination credential with an *active*, *inactive*, or *retired* status. Upon transfer of the ministerial credential, the receiving area conference shall be solely responsible for maintaining the credential through its supervision and accountability structure.

Ministers ordained in other Christian faith traditions

Mennonite Church Canada and Mennonite Church USA national offices will use the Placement Protocol discernment process to help a person from another Christian faith tradition to assess whether the person will thrive in the context of an Anabaptist/Mennonite congregation. If it seems good to the area conference minister and the national-church office then the person will be invited to fill out the Ministerial Leadership Information form and follow the standard process.

Ministers ordained in other Christian faith traditions who find a placement in Mennonite Church Canada or Mennonite Church USA will usually be given a two-year license credential, which may be renewed for an additional two years. A pastoral mentor will be assigned. Such a licensing period allows for discerning if the ministry relationship is beneficial to both the church and the ministering person. The licensed person will be expected to affirm and teach Anabaptist/Mennonite faith after doing prescribed study and reading in Mennonite history, theology, and ecclesiology. The person is expected to attend area-conference sessions and as pastoral-peer groups as a way to build relationships with other pastors, other congregations, and the area conference. Following the positive completion of the licensing period, a covenant ceremony led by the area conference will take place to affirm the person's previous ordination. A Mennonite certificate of ordination will be granted by the area conference.

The Calling and Locating of Pastors

Persons in pastoral ministry are members of the congregation where they serve and thus a part of the broader church and its life. They receive their call through the local congregation in consultation with the area conference and are accountable to the broader church through the area conference in which they reside.

The call to ministry

Potential pastors have a sense of call to serve Christ and the church effectively. A vital, living faith in Christ and a deep desire for the well-being of the church are essential. A person sensing a call from God to ministry also listens to the discernment of the church regarding his or her gifts for ministry. Congregations are active in identifying and encouraging men and women to consider pastoral ministry through shoulder tapping, praying for them, and encouraging them in their personal and spiritual development as they discern God's call. Congregations will also offer opportunities for experience to test these gifts in the congregation's missional activities.

Persons who sense a call to ministry prepare themselves through studies that relate to Mennonite Church Canada and Mennonite Church USA's identified six core competencies (biblical story, Anabaptist theology, Christian spirituality, self-awareness, missional engagement, and leadership). Those in oversight positions encourage these persons to grow in these competencies through formal and informal educational opportunities developed in our schools, area conferences, and national churches.

The ministerial leadership information (MLI) process

The national ministerial-leadership offices of Mennonite Church Canada and Mennonite Church USA work closely with area conferences to assist congregations in finding pastors. A person interested in a ministry position will complete the following steps:

1. Fill out an online MLI inquiry with the appropriate national office, or call the national office to express interest.

2. Following a conversation, the national office will assign access information for the MLI. This is usually done online.

3. Once the MLI is completed and submitted, and payment is made, the national office will process the form and send a reference form to persons named as references in the MLI. When the forms are returned, a composite of the responses will be developed.

4. Both national offices maintain a national registry of persons seeking a pastoral position. Area conferences have access to this list and may request an MLI, including references, for a congregational search committee within the area conference.

5. Persons seeking a position are encouraged to have contact with area-conference ministers to talk about possible openings. Each national office also keeps an online listing of congregations looking for a new pastor.

Finding the right place

Each area conference establishes procedures for helping those in pastoral ministry and congregations find a good fit for ministry. Congregations, like pastors, have personalities, gifts, particular challenges, missional callings, and histories. Therefore, careful consideration is given in the calling of a pastor. In the discernment process, attention is given to the pastoral gifts and the needs of the congregation. Much prayer and intentional work is required. (See the "Ministry Transition Packet" from the national ministerial-leadership offices of Mennonite Church Canada or Mennonite Church USA.)

Area-conference personnel are very important to this process. The area-conference minister or other conference personnel are fully involved in these times of transition. They encourage the congregation to consider both women and men for pastoral positions.

1. Ethics in Calling a Pastor

Congregational leaders follow area-conference guidelines in calling a pastor. They work carefully through area-conference structures before contacting or calling a person who is a pastor in another congregation in the same area, in the same conference, or elsewhere in the Mennonite church.

The call to a pastor is extended based on his/her credentials, without limitations based on gender, age, physical disabilities, or ethnic, cultural, and national identities. Persons who have experienced ethical or moral failure are considered seriously as candidates only after a careful discernment process guided by the area conference to determine the person's readiness for an active ministry role. Area conferences are responsible for sharing honest appraisal about their pastors who are seeking an assignment in another area conference.

Congregational leaders initiate honest conversations with the candidate about the process and how a call will finally be determined. They will always work at facilitating a good relationship between the candidate and the congregation.

2. Preparing a Memo of Understanding (Covenant of Agreement)

a. **Ministry descriptions.** Clear, written expectations agreeable to both the pastor and congregation will include the following: job description, time commitment, title, accountability, support structures, process for planning review and feedback, honoraria, and availability during vacation. A specified day off each week and a sabbatical policy also will be established.

Expectations are realistic, not excessive. This document is reviewed and revised annually to reflect changing expectations.

b. **Salary and benefits.** The salary paid to the pastor is proportionate to the pastor's training, experience, and responsibilities; the salary is also appropriate for the local cost of living. Salary is reviewed annually in consultation with the pastor. Our national-church offices set suggested salary guidelines for pastors, which congregations consult to set the pastor's salary and benefits.

c. **Term of service.** In some congregations, the understood term of service is for three or four years. In others, the term of service is open ended with no set length presumed. The Memo of Understanding (or Covenant of Agreement) should specify expectations.

d. **Outside requests.** Requests that fall outside the congregational pastoral work should be reviewed jointly by the pastor and congregational leaders. This includes requests to serve on local or national boards and requests from nonmembers for services such as funerals and weddings.

e. **Additional employment and activities.** Where the pastor serves full time, additional employment and other activities that take significant amounts of time are processed with congregational leadership before decisions are made. Should differences arise, counsel is sought from the area-conference personnel. In many settings ministry opportunities provide less than full-time employment. In such cases workloads are adjusted as appropriate. If the pastor chooses another part-time vocation, it will be consistent with the congregation's beliefs and will not interfere with pastoral responsibilities. The congregation will respect the part-time arrangement they have with the pastor and not put unrealistic full-time expectations on the pastor's time.

3. Pastor-Congregation Relationships

The ongoing health of the pastor-congregation relationship is of vital importance to the mission of the church. Many congregations find it helpful to establish a Pastor-Congregation Relations Committee or some other structure that tends to the relationship between the pastor and the congregation. In any support structure, the relationship is one of mutual counsel, support, and ongoing feedback.

In a time of personal crisis for the pastor, the congregational leaders go the second mile: offering love, trust, and personal support for the pastor and family, and adjusting the workload accordingly. The area-conference minister is notified immediately in order to access additional resources, counsel, and support. Similarly, a review process can be a time of significant stress for the pastor and family. Congregational leaders and area-conference personnel provide pastoral care during this time. The area conference will also provide congregational care in times of struggle and crisis.

4. Relating to a New Pastor

When a new pastor enters a congregation, a new relationship is established with the congregational leaders. Congregational leaders focus carefully on the new relationship, avoiding behavior or activities that hinder the development of the new relationship. Congregational leaders shape congregational behavior that permits the relationship with the previous pastor to lapse. Specifically, this means that the former pastor declines invitations from congregational members to have the former pastor officiate at weddings or funerals; the congregational leaders place all pastoral-care dynamics firmly in the hands of the new pastor. By providing such leadership, the congregational leaders create an environment in which members of the congregation will more readily transfer their love and support to the new pastor. The area conference will assist the congregation and previous pastor to develop a healthy covenant/agreement that will be beneficial to all involved. This should be done when the former pastor ends ministry in the congregation. Former and retired pastors have the responsibility to assist a smooth transition for the new pastor and support the pastor's ministry.

Relationships That Provide Resources for Ministry

Pastoral ministry involves personal commitment, acknowledgment, and joy that one is part of something larger than oneself. All pastors need a structure that provides resources and accountability to thrive in their calling. Pastors will become involved in relationships with groups or individuals—such as pastor-peer groups, spiritual directors, and prayer partners—in order to deepen their calling and connection to God's purposes in the world. Pastors will also attend to their relationship with God, spouse, and family. Alignment of one's calling to God's vision for the world, though not easy, is full of deep purpose and joy.

Pastoral accountability to the appropriate congregational leaders and area-conference personnel—as well as attendance at wider church gatherings—is also a means to receive support and direction for remaining faithful to God's call. Reports and reviews to those to whom one is responsible are to be understood as positive and healthy.

Preparation for leadership ministry

Persons called to ministry are disciples of Christ, constant learners in fulfilling their vocational call. Both specific preparation and continued learning are essential for ministry to be sustained and effective. Area-conference ministers are aware of, and promote, various ways in which the six core competencies (biblical story, Anabaptist theology, Christian spirituality, self-awareness, missional engagement, and leadership) can be pursued for persons in ministry. Our Mennonite schools and some area conferences offer training in a variety of formats: traditional residential classes, online and hybrid classes, credit and no credit classes, and correspondence classes. While the standard ministry degree (master of divinity) is preferred, the person's continued desire for growth is of greater interest. The time of licensing allows for specific courses to be taken, as suggested by the credentialing body, to focus on one or more of the core competencies. Congregations and other ministry locations where the pastor serves are encouraged to provide financial support for this work.

Pastoral review

A pastoral review and other forms of informal response are inevitable, natural, and always present. For healthy ministry and congregational life, a formal review will be designed by the pastor, congregational leaders, and area-conference leaders. It will be conducted with the consultation of area-conference personnel. Informal or ill-prepared reviews are unfair, play into fears and threats of particular persons, and disrespect the pastor. Only reviews designed according to the congregation's stated goals and priorities and the pastor's job description will be effective in bringing the desired ends for growth.

The goal is to conduct a formal review in a responsible manner that contributes to the health and well-being of both the congregation and the pastor. The basic purpose of a pastoral review is to facilitate growth toward more effective ministry, affirm the areas that are going well, and bless the pastor. The pastor and the congregation are best served when the review has an eye for the future rather than the past. The review will affirm areas of strength and identify areas of growth.

It is unwise to undertake a review process when other major issues are being addressed by the congregation or area conference. If significant conflicts are present, they should be addressed separately and prior to any formal review.

Along with a review of the pastor, it is appropriate to do a congregational review that assesses current reality, clarifies priorities, and establishes goals to pursue in participating in God's mission in the world. Working with area-conference leaders is strongly encouraged to offer resources and perspectives as the review is designed, carried out, and processed.

Search for Wholeness in Ministry

Pastors are personally aware of God's grace in their lives and give out of the abundance of that grace. Their ongoing attention to spiritual, emotional, physical, familial, and social health contributes to a healthy ministry and a healthy church. Each person in ministry will take responsibility to work at wholeness for self and encourage wholeness in others.

Section IV: Ethics in Ministry

Ethics for pastors, congregational leaders, area-conference and national staff, chaplains, and others in ministry beyond the congregation are based on a covenant relationship with God through Jesus Christ. This covenant is renewed at the Lord's Supper. It is formed with Christ and the church at baptism, and it is strengthened through every moment of grace experienced in Christ's body.

Ethical standards are set to create and maintain loving, caring, and responsible relationships within the church so that the church will be empowered to effectively participate in Christ's ministry. Adherence to ethical standards also enhances the individual's life and ministry.

General Principles of Accountability

Accountability for congregational leaders

Congregational leaders have accountability systems within the congregation where they serve. Job descriptions provide clarity about responsibilities and duties. Regular reviews of their work provide feedback and accountability as well as support. Congregational leaders are encouraged to take advantage of opportunities for fellowship and learning experiences provided by the area conference and wider church.

Accountability for pastors

Persons in pastoral ministry develop multiple accountability relationships with congregational leaders and the area conference that holds their ministry credential. A memo of understanding (see page 48) addresses job description; regular settings for mutual feedback, nurture, reference, counsel, and support; and the process and intention of ministry reviews. Review can be initiated by either the pastor or congregational leaders. Principles that guide both pastor and congregational leaders include the health of the congregation, sensitivity to the pastor's needs, and concern not to injure individuals or contribute to the failure of the pastor's ministry. Pastors serving on a pastoral team also have a covenant of understanding that will guide the accountability and work between them.

The pastor realizes that the congregation is part of the wider church. The pastor recognizes the mutual support and resourcing given and received from the area conference and national church. Together they work for God's kingdom.

Accountability for ministers in area-conference and national offices

Persons called to these church offices are accountable to both the congregation in which they hold membership and to the area conference that holds their credential. Area-conference ministers also are accountable to their peers in other area conferences through regular gatherings, which provide counsel and encouragement. All area-conference leaders must be accountable to a leadership-credentialing body that establishes written agreements defining what accountability means in their particular area conference.

Accountability for intentional, transitional, and interim supply pastors

Area-conference ministers often encourage the use of an intentional, transitional, or interim supply pastor during a pastoral transition in the life of a congregation. This gives the congregation space and opportunity to work on a number of items such as grief, loss, internal conflict, and pain; to seek clarity about the congregation's mission; to strengthen the health of the congregation; and to prepare for a new pastor. Intentional, transitional, and interim supply pastors may move to provide this specialized ministry in a congregation belonging to another area conference, but their credential remains in their "home" area conference, where they are accountable to the leadership-credentialing body. Specialized pastors are also accountable to the area conference in which they are serving.

Accountability for chaplains and others in ministry beyond the congregation

Persons called in these areas have accountability as an employee of their institutions. They are guided by the job description for their assignment. They are also accountable to both the Mennonite congregation in which they hold membership and to the area conference that holds their credential. A covenant of understanding for accountability and support is to be developed between the person, their congregation, and the area conference so as to offer guidance and support in these relationships. These persons are held to the same standards of ethics as those in pastoral ministry.

Ethics Related to the Pastoral Office

The candidate process

The potential pastor takes the initiative to learn about the process that will be undertaken as he or she begins the candidate relationship with a congregation. The candidate is careful to respect the congregation's process at each step. If a person who is not a member of the congregation's search committee approaches the candidate about the search process, the candidate directs the member to the search committee. The pastoral candidate exercises confidentiality and care when seeking counsel and consults with the area-conference minister. During the search process, the candidate is encouraged to establish a confidential support group for him- or herself.

Relationship to other congregational leaders

The pastor is one leader among the leadership of a congregation. The pastor works with congregational leaders to discover the congregation's role in tending God's mission in the community. With this shared vision the pastor leads, inspiring and empowering the congregation to be God's people and to witness through trust and collaboration. The vision and goals of the congregation guide how the pastor uses his or her time—being accountable to congregational leaders, keeping them informed, and regularly consulting with them. In decision making and times of conflict, the best gifts the pastor can offer are an impartial, non-anxious presence and an Anabaptist theological framework. The pastor takes responsibility to ensure that the congregation remains connected and involved with the area conference and national church.

Resignation and leaving a pastoral assignment

The pastor will process any decision around resignation and ending a pastoral assignment with the area-conference minister and the appropriate leaders of the congregation prior to any public announcement. Together they will determine a clearly stated ending date (three to six months is considered appropriate) that respects the commitment made in the covenant of understanding when the pastor began. The period between the announcement and the final day is an important time of bringing closure and ending well so that the congregation is freed to consider their future with a new leader. The pastor will refrain from giving leadership to that future. Both pastor and congregation are encouraged to plan a significant ending of blessing so both can move on to the next phase of life.

After leaving a pastoral assignment

When the pastoral assignment is finished and the pastor moves on to another role or retires, the pastor gives the former congregation and its new leader space to form a new pastor-congregation relationship. The former pastor exercises great sensitivity to his or her successor and refrains from returning to the congregation to provide leadership. The reappearance of a former pastor at times of crisis or life-transition interferes with the normal development of the relationships between members and the new pastor. Pastoral care is left in the hands of one's successor. Invitations to participate in weddings and funerals are declined—except in rare occasions when a former pastor considers an invitation at the request of the current pastor. The best pastoral care offered by a former pastor is to attend the event rather than exercising public leadership. Return visits to the congregation are infrequent and casual.

There are contexts which the former pastor will stay in the community and continue to be a member of the congregation where he or she was the pastor. The former pastor's attendance at church activities during the first 12 months of a new pastor's arrival is discouraged. This practice is important to give the congregation space to move forward with new leadership. In this situation the former pastor is proactive in assuring the new pastor of his or her support and respect, and shows willingness to be part of an accountability group for the former pastor if requested by the congregational or area-conference leaders. The new pastor and area-conference personnel give leadership to this accountability group. This group will help navigate the former pastor's new relationship with the congregation in a way that respects and supports the new pastor's transition into the congregation. The former pastor is responsible to this group for his or her relating in the congregation and only accepts ministry invitations at the request of the current pastor.

There are cultural contexts with different understandings about the role of former pastors. The goal, however, is healthy leadership relationships that help the congregation continue to focus on joining God's mission in the world.

Ethical Practice for Pastoral Ministry

"Article 15: Ministry and Leadership" in *Confession of Faith in a Mennonite Perspective* states, "The character and reputation of leaders is to be above reproach." Leaders are to follow the example of Christ in all they do "so that the church may be 'built together spiritually into a dwelling place for God.'" Leaders who maintain a healthy spiritual life, healthy personal relationships, and a solid accountability structure will find the support needed to discern the ethical issues that face them in their ministry.

Use of power

To varying degrees, all pastors are given power in the congregations they serve. This power is both given by the congregation and held by the pastor. To deny this power is to misuse a sacred trust that has been extended to them. A pastor seeks to be authoritative rather than authoritarian. In times of conflict or controversy, the pastor receives counsel both within and outside the congregation to discern whether the issue belongs to the congregation, is a reflection on his or her leadership, or is a combination of both.

It is necessary to acknowledge one's own limitations as well as those of others. The pastor avoids favoritism, or building a group around him- or herself. The pastor refrains from cultivating a "lone ranger" style, but rather seeks to enhance cooperation and interdependence with other leaders in the congregation. The stance is *our* church rather than *my* church.

The pastor models appropriate administrative behavior, passes on information, offers counsel and support, and maintains a stance of care, accuracy, and competence. The pastor trusts the congregation's decision-making ability and brings an appropriate theological perspective to that process. The role is that of both guide and facilitator.

In the congregation the pastor is not the only person with power. The pastor will soon discover persons with economic, societal, and even historic power in the congregation. Understanding and naming the realities of various powers is important for a pastor to work within the local ministry context.

Family relationships

The pastor seeks to maintain a healthy balance between church, family, and friends. He or she models healthy ways to set aside the pastoral role while spending time with family and friends. Such relationships are vital in emotional health and spiritual vitality while offering pastoral leadership in a congregation. While friendships within the congregation may be possible, the pastor must be clear about his or her pastoral role. It is therefore helpful to also form friendships outside the congregational setting.

If a pastor is married, the pastor's spouse is encouraged to develop his or her own sense of identity, and to maintain clarity about this separate identity with the congregational leaders. The pastor's work demands are balanced with adequate spousal and family time.

The well-being of the pastor's marital relationship becomes important to the congregation as well. Ongoing marital tensions affect not only the family involved but also the ministry of the pastor and eventually the congregation. In such situations the area-conference leadership should be made aware and become an appropriate source for finding support. In the event of a separation or divorce, it is advisable for the area conference and congregation to negotiate with the pastor a time away from pastoral duties for a season of healing. The area conference and congregation will be involved in further discernment about the pastor's ongoing ministry.

Single pastors who choose to date are encouraged to form a dating relationship with someone from another congregation. Should mutual interest in a dating relationship begin with an individual in the congregation where the pastor is serving, the pastor must be open and honest about this relationship with the area-conference minister and congregational leaders. The pastor will show a willingness to follow their counsel for the well-being of the congregation and the dating relationship.

Self-care

A pastor's ability to provide pastoral care for others is based on appropriate self-care: taking time for physical well-being, appropriate support and accountability systems, spiritual direction, counseling, and strong family relationships. The pastor talks with congregational leadership when one's own needs and congregational expectations are getting out of balance. A pastor will have a strong work ethic and also a strong practice of Sabbath keeping and rest to avoid either laziness or overfunctioning.

Accumulated crises can create great personal stress. The pastor should be aware of the value of seeking the support and counsel of a pastoral peer or the area-conference minister. Realistic appraisal of one's own needs and written understandings about support systems within the congregation can alleviate some of the stress. The pastor desires to continually learn about his or her context, his or her vocational calling, and Scripture. Regular practices in the Christian disciplines are vitally important to nurture the heart of a ministering person.

Sexuality

Our deepest longings for God are related to our needs for intimacy with other human beings. The spiritual yearnings that energize us for ministry are related to our sexuality. Pastors need to be clear about appropriate relationships and boundary issues. Celibacy is the standard for single persons and a monogamous, heterosexual relationship for married persons, as reflected in Article 19 of our Confession of Faith in a Mennonite Perspective.[1]

Truth telling

All church leaders are responsible to model and coach others to speak the truth in love, avoiding the tendency to *triangle* others into one's concerns (telling another person what one should rightly say to the person who is directly involved). A leader does not repeat the complaint to others on behalf of the person offended, but rather helps the person offended to speak the truth for him- or herself. Congregational leaders encourage members to speak directly with the pastor about concerns related to the pastor, rather than speaking indirectly about the pastor through the congregational leaders. In almost all cases, Jesus' instructions about going first to the brother or sister who has been the offender (Matthew 18:15-20) are the basis for such truth telling. When there is a power difference between the pastor and the individual, a contact person will be appointed by congregational leaders to accompany the person to talk with the pastor. When an individual makes a complaint of pastoral or leadership abuse, the *Ministerial Sexual Misconduct Policy and Procedure* instructs how truth telling will be addressed.

---

1   In separate resolutions that were adopted in 2015 by Mennonite Church USA (On the Status of the Membership Guidelines and Forbearance in the Midst of Differences) and in 2016 by Mennonite Church Canada (Being a Faithful Church 7: Summary and recommendation on sexuality, 2009-2015), both denominations reaffirmed their commitment to the position articulated by the *Confession of Faith in a Mennonite Perspective*. In those same resolutions, both denominations acknowledged that not all agree to this stance, and offered forbearance or space for discernment for congregations who may choose a different way. However, before blessing same-sex marriages, such congregations are expected to prayerfully discern God's will for their situation, and to cooperate fully with the policies or guidelines of their Area Churches or Area Conferences.

The pastor speaks the truth about him- or herself, refraining from exaggeration or deception about credentials, training, experience, past record, finances, convictions of crime, or ethical misconduct. Consultation and discernment with area-conference leadership is vital when determining how and what the pastor needs to share about past or current struggles—so that the pastor is not trapped by the destructive power of secrecy, but rather speaks with integrity and wisdom concerning what the congregation needs to know.

Similarly, area-conference ministers must have integrity in their consultations. Such integrity is found by honestly sharing information about hard-to-place pastoral candidates, by sharing information with other area conferences or national churches, and by forthrightness with pastoral candidates who are not suited to pastoral ministry.

Confidentiality

Confidentiality is about respect and care for the information received through the work of the office of pastor. It is not secret keeping. Pastors request permission when sharing information with others in the congregation about an individual's situation, health, or family. There are times when a pastor must share confidential information with others: when child abuse is suspected or when people are at risk of hurting themselves or others. Beyond these special circumstances, a pastor seeks to work with individuals to receive their consent when additional resources and people would be helpful to the situation and ministry.

Pastors and congregational leaders are intentional about developing understandings with each other around what is appropriately shared in a congregational leaders' meeting. They model and share their understanding of confidentiality and information sharing with the congregation. This helps the congregation to follow safe and healthy practices for respecting personal information, whether in face-to-face settings or through electronic or social media.

Impartiality

Pastors seek to serve all persons from the congregation with impartiality, recognizing that one cannot pastor everyone. Area-conference ministers, when working with confidential personnel information, need to deal justly and impartially with all pastoral candidates and congregations.

Relationship of the area conference to the pastor and congregation

The area conference provides resources to pastors, their families, and congregational leaders. These resources include counsel in pastoral search, interim leadership, and reviews; leadership development opportunities; support in times of crisis or conflict; and general encouragement of pastoral and congregational health. In matters relating to pastoral credentials, final responsibility rests with the area conference, which processes all issues in granting credentials for leadership ministry and in disciplinary actions related to them.

Preaching and teaching

Regular study of the Bible, reflection and praxis of core Anabaptist convictions, a life of discipleship built on prayer and guided by the Holy Spirit, as well as missional engagement—these form a solid basis for the pastor to faithfully interpret the Scriptures. The pastor is disciplined in engaging biblical texts from the whole Bible—including difficult and personally unattractive texts—and avoids overusing favorite themes. Preaching and teaching that is also open to the wisdom and insights of others equips the congregation for faithful living and witness. The foundation of preaching is Jesus Christ and God's revelation of the good news throughout the whole biblical text. The goal of preaching is for God's reign to be the lens through which we see and the way in which we live in the world. The pastor is aware of the privilege and authority of the preaching act. The pastor prayerfully and humbly guards against misuses of that privilege and authority—including preaching that is self-righteous or manipulative, that plagiarizes, or that reveals confidential information.

The pastor is encouraged to exercise prophetic freedom, recognizing that the congregation's ability to receive the message comes from a growing relationship of trust and respect. The pastor and congregation seek to live by the Sermon on the Mount and to address conflict with the model from Jesus' teaching in Matthew 18. The pastor will respect and be guided by the beliefs and practices of the Mennonite church. The pastor also recognizes his or her own limitations. The pastor invites and nurtures others for preaching and teaching so that the congregation is equipped through the five-fold ministry of leadership (Ephesians 4) for service and Christ-like maturity.

Pastoral care and counseling

The pastor leads the congregation in caring for one another. In pastoral care the pastor is aware of the power he or she has that comes from knowledge, experience, gender, race, social standing, physical presence, pastoral role, position, and authority.

Counseling focuses on helping the individual(s), couple, or family grow in wholeness and maturity as disciples and as part of the faith community. The pastor works confidentially, ensuring personal safety for both the counselee(s) and the pastor. The pastor recognizes his or her limitations and the value of referral. When a pastor counsels, it is for a limited number of sessions (usually not more than six). The pastor then refers to a professional counselor if further care is needed. The pastor is always responsible for the counseling relationship. Peer accountability and professional coaching can support the pastor in maintaining a healthy counseling relationship. Any sexualized behavior by the pastor in a counseling setting is totally unacceptable. Such behavior is a betrayal of trust, exploitative, abusive, and a sin. The pastor will be familiar with the *Ministerial Sexual Misconduct Policy and Procedure.*

Relationship to the community

The pastor faithfully represents the congregation in the community and gives leadership in equipping individuals and the congregation to be Christ's presence and witness in the community. The congregation's theology guides its public witness and action. The pastor acts as an advocate for ecumenical relationships and shapes the congregation's understandings of God's redeeming work and mission in the world. The pastor is respectful of others while recognizing faith distinctives. He or she seeks to enhance relationships among congregations in the local community, sharing resources as appropriate and assisting the congregation's self-understanding as part of God's diverse church.

The pastor and stress points

The pastor is aware of his or her capacity for ministry—including strengths and limitations—and that others have also been given gifts to be shared within the body (Romans 12:3-5). The pastor respects diversity, lives creatively with differences, manages stress, and takes clear stands without imposing his or her convictions on others. When differences arise the pastor is motivated by genuine love for the other and by "what is good" (Romans 12:9-10) to address the difference. When congregational conflict arises, the pastor and congregational leaders follow the ethics of truth telling (Matthew 18) and contact the area conference for assistance.

Technology and the pastor

Advancements in technology, such as the Internet and social media, have become an important tool for ministry. Those same advancements in technology have also brought new challenges with age-old issues such as pornography, marital infidelity, and plagiarism. With faith as the guiding foundation and attention to one's power and professional boundaries, the healthy pastor will discern together with congregational leaders as to what is appropriate use of technology and accountability for its use.

When Covenant Relationships Are Broken

Sometimes a relationship develops between a pastor and individual, whether a child or an adult, that is not appropriate. This may include unusual attention given or received by a pastor, including such things as gifts, emails, other social media contact, telephone calls, letters, private visits, and the maintenance of a special "spiritualized" partnership. These inappropriate relationships result in great pain and grief for the victim, families, and the congregation. It is imperative that the pastor resist every temptation to develop such inappropriate relationships. Because of the power and authority implicit in the ministerial office, such inappropriate relating constitutes sexual harassment and abuse. No matter how this misconduct begins, it is always the pastor's responsibility to stop this behavior.

Pastor sexual misconduct includes, but is not limited to:
- flirtations, advances, or propositions
- conversations and shared images—electronic or otherwise—of a sexual nature
- graphic or degrading comments about another person's appearance, dress, or anatomy
- display of sexually suggestive objects or pictures
- sexual jokes, innuendos, and offensive gestures
- sexual or intrusive questions about a person's personal life
- explicit descriptions of the minister's own sexual experiences

- abuse of familiarities or diminutives such as "honey," "baby," or "dear"
- unnecessary, unwanted physical contact such as touching, hugging, pinching, patting, or kissing
- whistling, catcalls
- leering
- exposing genitalia
- physical or sexual assault
- sexual intercourse or rape

To guard against self-delusion in such matters, area-conference ministers will work with pastors proactively with teachings and practices for healthy boundaries. Pastors will regularly reflect on their own vulnerability and temptations and will seek appropriate accountability relationships. When needed, area-conference ministers will make referrals and consultations for support, counsel, and therapy.

There are times when a credentialed person abuses the trust placed in him or her by the congregation. Such abuse damages the covenant relationship between the congregation, its leaders, the credentialed person, and the wider church. Individuals who become aware of misconduct by a credentialed person will contact the area-conference office. The area-conference office will follow the steps outlined in the *Ministerial Sexual Misconduct Policy and Procedure*. This document can also be used for a variety of other ministerial-misconduct situations with minimal adaptations. The following examples are breaches of trust by a credentialed person that will initiate the review process:

- violations of confidentiality
- use of technology for illegal or immoral purposes
- pornography
- intentional deceptions or dishonesty, including misrepresentation of self in training or past records
- acts of physical, emotional, or spiritual violence

- gross neglect of ministerial responsibilities
- financial irresponsibility or irregularities
- sexual abuse, sexual violence, or sexual harassment
- failure to be accountable to the area conference that holds the credential
- major theological deviation from Christian and Anabaptist/Mennonite understandings
- the effort to harm the leadership of another pastor
- behaviors that undermine the congregation, another congregation, or the relationship with the wider Mennonite church.

Area-conference ministers will work with pastors proactively with teachings and practices for healthy boundaries. Pastors will regularly reflect on their own vulnerability and temptations and will seek appropriate accountability relationships. When needed, area-conference ministers will make referrals and consultations for support, counsel, and therapy.

Final words of encouragement

As was stated in the introduction, this book is to name a common understanding of ministerial leadership in Mennonite Church Canada and Mennonite Church USA. It is not intended to be a rule book, nor is there any assumption that every possible ministry question is addressed in these pages. It is, however, our effort to build lasting relationships of respect and integrity between congregations, area conferences, and their credentialed leaders. Area conferences have a commitment to be consistent and accountable to each other for the sake of encouraging healthy leaders and congregations. This commitment includes a willingness to address new issues in our ever-changing and complex church as together we come to a deeper understanding of God's call on the life of the church.

Be shepherds of God's flock that is under your care,
watching over them—not because you must,
but because you are willing, as God wants you to be;
not pursuing dishonest gain, but eager to serve;
not lording it over those entrusted to you,
but being examples to the flock.
—1 Peter 5:2-3 (NIV)

Glossary of Terms

Accountability: A relationship in which a person credentialed for ministry voluntarily subjects his or her actions and ministry to a person or group that carries authority to represent the church.

Area Conference: A regional body of Mennonite congregations covenanting together for purposes of mission, fellowship, and credentialing. Together, they make up the national churches. This term describes *conferences* of Mennonite Church USA and *area churches* of Mennonite Church Canada.

Area-Conference Minister: An oversight minister, at the area-conference level, who serves as pastor to regional ministers, overseers and/or pastors. Significant duties include linking pastors and congregations, overseeing credentialing, arranging for mentors, and organizing clusters of pastors. *Area-conference* describes conferences of Mennonite Church USA and area churches of Mennonite Church Canada.

Bishop: A term used by some area conferences for a person whose office emphasizes spiritual oversight of ministers (pastors), and often of congregations.

Bi-vocational Pastor: A pastor employed less than full time in a ministry position, with another vocation or job. A pastor is always a minister even if he or she spends some time on another job.

Chaplaincy: One form of credentialed ministry in settings such as schools, hospitals, prisons, and retirement homes.

Church: The term *church* refers to the wider body of Mennonite Church Canada and Mennonite Church USA, who have covenanted together through area conferences and national churches. The church is also a global reality that includes Mennonite World Conference and other Christian faith traditions.

Confession of Faith: This refers to a statement of Anabaptist beliefs and understandings that guide the faith and life of Mennonite Church Canada and Mennonite Church USA. The current confession of faith is entitled *Confession of Faith in a Mennonite Perspective* (1995).

Congregation: The local community of believers in a specific place, covenanted together for worship, fellowship, and mission.

Covenant: In the faith community, covenant is understood as an agreement built on promises made in the presence of God. Covenants are made between pastor and congregation, between the congregation and area conference, and between the area conference and national church.

Credential: A designation of rights and privileges for a person serving in a ministry role within Mennonite Church Canada or Mennonite Church USA.

Deacon: In some congregations, deacons serve as support to the pastor and help plan the spiritual ministry of the congregation. Some are involved in worship leading, preaching, counseling, conflict resolution, discipline, benevolence ministry, etc. The term *deacon* includes both men and women.

Denomination: The larger-church body of a particular Christian tradition. In this document Mennonite Church Canada and Mennonite Church USA are considered partner denominations.

Discipline: Measures taken to hold a credentialed person accountable for breaking ethical or moral standards.

Elder: This term is used to describe the role of congregational leaders other than the pastor (including deacons and lay ministers).

File/Profile: A record about a credentialed person, maintained by national-office staff through MennoData. It includes, but is not limited to, the Ministerial Leadership Information form, references, and pastor status.

Intentional Interim, Transitional Pastor: The terms *intentional* and *transitional* are used interchangeably as well as together but mean the same thing. This type of pastor helps the congregation set a new vision, direction, and way of working together that either enhances health or brings health to a congregation.

Interim Supply Pastor: This term designates a person who takes a short-term assignment in ministry in a congregation that is between pastors. A supply pastor is one who comes in to maintain basic ministry.

Lay Ministry: Ministry usually done without pay and without formal training, on a marginal-time basis. Lay ministers may have been ordained in the past but more commonly now are commissioned by the congregation. They normally make their living at another occupation.

MennoData: A system is used by both Mennonite Church Canada and Mennonite Church USA for managing the records of pastors, pastoral credentials, congregations, and area conferences. It also holds the Ministerial Leadership Information form for individuals looking for new or first pastoral positions, or preparing for a ministerial credential. The online directory for Mennonite Church USA is generated from the MennoData system.

Ministerial Credentialing, Competencies, and Education: The *six core competencies* identified by area-conference leaders as required in pastoral leaders within congregations of Mennonite Church Canada and Mennonite Church USA. These are biblical story, Anabaptist theology, Christian spirituality, self-awareness, missional engagement, and leadership.

Ministerial Leadership Information Form (MLI): The instrument used by the ministerial calling system of Mennonite Church Canada and Mennonite Church USA to gather personal, training, ministry, and theological information about a student or pastor who desires a ministry placement.

Ministry in Specialized Settings: Ministry in noncongregational settings such as schools, hospitals, prisons, and retirement homes. This ministry is usually provided by ordained persons.

National Office: Mennonite Church Canada or Mennonite Church USA staff.

Office of Ministerial Leadership: The national office of either Mennonite Church Canada or Mennonite Church USA. It provides resources for congregations and pastors, and networking for area conferences. This office also provides support for area-conference personnel.

Overseer: In some area conferences, a pastor or area-conference leader is appointed to provide oversight to congregations and pastors. Overseers are usually discerned and appointed for a specific term by congregations, pastors, and conference leadership commissions. There are variations from area conference to area conference in the practical details of this office and its ministry.

Polity: The ministerial structure within Mennonite Church Canada and Mennonite Church USA, as well the policies, understandings, and practices to guide leadership ministry.

Specialized Ministries See *Ministry in Specialized Settings.*

Index

77

Find supporting resources at the website of Mennonite Church Canada (home.mennonitechurch.ca) or Mennonite Church USA (www.mennoniteusa.org):

- On Mennonite Church Canada's homepage, click on the "What We Do" tab, and select "Pastoral Leadership." (For the *Confession of Faith in a Mennonite Perspective*, click on the "About" tab, and select "Beliefs.")
- On Mennonite Church USA's homepage, click on the "Resource Center" tab, and select "Information about Mennonites," "Leadership Development," or "Pastors."

Mennonite Church Canada
600 Shaftesbury Blvd.
Winnipeg, MB R3P 0M4
866-888-6785

Mennonite Church USA
3145 Benham Ave., Suite 1
Elkhart, IN 46517
OR
718 N. Main St.
Newton, KS 67114-1703
866-866-2872